Taxes:

Everything You Need to Know About Taxes For Your Small Business — Sole Proprietorship, Startup, & LLC

Harry Monroe

D1279576

Table Of Contents

Introduction

It has been said in life, two things that are definite — death and taxes. In business, there is only one that is definite: taxes. Tax requirements go hand-in-hand with managing a business. From the federal level all the way down to city hall, you will need to be responsible for knowing what taxes to pay for your business, when you need to file them and make sure you file on time. Make a mistake or miss a deadline and your business will suffer consequences known as penalties.

Taxes are one of the least favorite subjects for small business owners. However, it's one of the most vital topics for your business. The steps you take before the end of the tax year will facilitate your business's ability to save money on the amount of taxes you owe. The start of the next tax year is the best time to evaluate whether or not you're capitalizing on your deductions and perhaps even getting a second look at extra deductions that will allow you to save money for your business. Recognizing a method to curtail the quantity of taxes you pay means that you will be able to retain a lot of the money you make. Fall short of accurately controlling your taxes, and your business may have hassles finishing up.

As you become a small business owner, you gain a liability for creating tax payments that you simply did not have as an employee. As an employee, your boss was transmitting your part of the taxes and withheld them from your paycheck to send to the government. The corporation was additionally matching your Social Security and Medicare taxes, cutting the cost for you in half, and was at the same time filing info returns to the Internal Revenue Service.

Taxes are compulsory expenses for any company, and there are no two ways about it. Whether you like it or not, you have to pay taxes in order to avoid running into problems with the IRS.

However, when it comes to paying taxes, many companies remain unaware of what really needs to be done. Despite having filed taxes through several years, businesses don't put in efforts to understand why they are paying these taxes and forgo other generic information on the topic.

Knowing what or why something is being done gives people an advantage, and will give you one as well, provided you go through it in detail. In fact, it is possible for small business owners to reduce the amount of tax that they need to pay, by capitalizing on some of the tax saving schemes.

The US tax system can be a little tricky since there are many forms and schedules to be aware of. And it might seem a little harrowing for a new business owner to pay the tax for the first year of the company.

This book will act as your true taxation guide and usher you into the right direction. The main purpose will be to demonstrate what tax provisions you will be held liable for as a small business owner.

I thank you for choosing this book and hope you have a good time reading it.

Chapter 1

Tax Basics

In this first chapter, we will look at the different questions that get asked on the subject of taxes, and answer them to help you understand the topic better.

What are taxes?

It is common knowledge that taxes are compulsory expenses that are levied by the government on a person's income, a company's profits or on the sale of goods and services. This money is diverted to the government, who use it for the upkeep of the overall economy. The federal government uses the money for many reasons such as providing relief to the poor, maintaining the streets, providing pension to retired government employees etc. Taxes are a part and parcel of any company and it is extremely important for them to pay their dues on time.

Who levies them?

Different institutions levy taxes at different levels. The federal government will levy a tax on your company regardless of where you are based. The city tax is levied by your city council. County tax is levied on a company that belongs to a particular county and state tax is levied on a company based on the state that it belongs to. So there is no any one institution that levies a tax on a company different bodies that levy them. All of them, however, are governed by the IRS.

Are taxes universally applicable?

The concept of taxes is universally applicable but the amount to be paid will differ from company to company. There is no universal tax amount that is levied and how much will be levied depends on several factors. You have to know which tax slab your company belongs to and pay the taxes accordingly. In fact, some small businesses might be exempt from paying taxes owing to earning small revenue.

Are there deadlines to paying taxes?

Yes, there are deadlines to paying taxes and it is important to pay everything before the last date. Not paying on time will invite unnecessary fines. The deadline for filing taxes is generally April 15th, within which date you are required to file and return your taxes. It is possible for you to extend it to April 18th if you have not yet filled out all the forms.

Are there benefits to filing early?

Yes. There are many benefits to filing early. For one, you will not feel stressed at the last minute and would have finished all the formalities well in advance. You might also have the chance to save on some of the taxes that you have to pay. You can also avoid the risk of having to pay a fine if you end up surpassing the last day to pay your taxes.

Is there a way to save on tax?

Yes, there are many ways to save on taxes. You can make use of tax deductions to save on the amount that you pay as taxes. For example, if you own an S Corp then you can deduct your health insurance. Sole proprietors can have medical expenses reimbursement, which will help them save on taxes. We will look at more of these in chapters to come.

Should I do it alone?

Not necessarily. You can take the help of a chartered accountant to file for taxes or a legal advisor. They will be able to help you fill out all the right forms and get you started on the right foot. It is also important for you to get your partners involved if you have a partnership firm. Sole proprietors might need a little extra help, especially if they are filing for the first time.

How much do they charge me?

How much the accountant or the advisor will charge you depends on how much work they are doing for you. If your accountant is doing everything for you from scratch, then you will have to shell out quite a lot. But if you have prepared the important documents to be submitted to the accountant then you might not have to spend too much. It is best for you to set aside a certain sum that you can use to pay your accountant. Most businesses set aside between $150 and $200, which they use to pay the accountant. But there is no one amount that can be finalized as it will vary from individual to individual.

How long does it take to file?

Preparing to file for taxes might take a little time. You have to ready the different papers and also collect the various bills that you will deduct from your tax. But the actual process of filing for taxes might not take any more than an hour or two. If you have been filing for a while then it might take just 10 minutes! It will be very easy if you take the help of a professional, as they will know what needs to be filled out and the right sequence to go about it. How much time it will take will depend on how fast you are at filling forms and how ready you are for it!

I have been filing income tax, is it the same?

Most of the procedures will be the same but the forms will be different. You will obviously have to fill out forms that are specific to companies. The forms might not be as inclusive as what corporates might have to fill out but will require you to provide quite a lot of information. Filing for income tax is sometimes viewed as an arduous task. But it will be arduous only if you think of it that way and not as a mandatory course of action that you have to take up, once a year.

Should sole proprietors also pay taxes?

Yes, they do. Sole proprietors that earn an income through employment must pay taxes to the IRS. How much is to be paid depends on how much you make.

These form some of the questions that get asked on the topic and hope you had yours answered as well.

Chapter 2
Types of Taxes Collected

There are many types of taxes that can be levied and you have to know them in order to successfully pay them. In this chapter, we will look at the main taxes that are levied on a business.

Federal taxes

The first and most important tax that you should know about is the federal tax. Federal taxes are imposed on small businesses, depending on how much profit they make. This tax will be different from what you will pay to your state. Federal taxes are possibly the biggest sum that you will pay, as the margin levied is quite large. In case of businesses that have employees, you have to submit employees' tax holdings along with payroll taxes and social security taxes. In order to pay your federal taxes, you will have to make use of the right forms, which are as follows.

Sole Proprietor: Form 1040 Schedule C or C-EZ and additionally Schedule F for a farm business.

Partnership: Form 1065 in order to submit profits and gains. Remember that a partnership firm only disburses its profits to partners.

C Corporations: Form 1120

S Corporations: Form 1120S

Limited Liability Company: Form 1040 with Schedules C, E and F.

You have to submit your forms 1020, 1020S and 1120A to the IRS by 15th March every year, for the previous year.

Form 1040, 1065 and Schedule C should be submitted to the IRS by April 15th.

It is extremely important for you to pay your federal taxes in case you want to avoid any problems.

State level taxes

State level taxes refer to the taxes that your particular state will levy on your business. Each and every individual state in the US has its very own laws, which means that you have to know your state's laws in detail in order to file for taxes.

The rules can vary for sole proprietor, LLC and startup firms. Based on the business that you are carrying out, you have to go through the different tax laws that your company might be subject to.

Apart from collecting company taxes, these states also collect sales taxes. Sales taxes are levied on the sale of products and services. If the company has bought goods for its operation from outside the state, then a tax will be levied on it as well. This type is better known as *use tax* and you have to pay it in order to avoid discrepancies.

However, if you as a company have bought goods for retail sale, then no taxes will be levied on it.

City taxes

City taxes are also levied on business by the city's government in order to operate legally. But this is always just a one-time expense for the business. In exchange, the company will get a legal permit and also government recognition, both of which are important for a company to fare well.

County taxes

County taxes are levied on those businesses that operate in a particular county. How much needs to be paid will depend on the rules set by the particular county. The tax is mostly levied on any vehicles, buildings or other physical goods that the company owns.

These form the different types of taxes that can be levied on your company by the IRS. You have to bear in mind that you will have to pay all of these and make room for them in your annual budget. If you have been filing taxes for some time now, then you will know to keep a substantial sum ready to direct towards taxes. But if this is your first year in paying taxes then you have to know to keep a particular sum aside to pay your taxes.

Chapter 3

Understanding the Internal Revenue System

In this chapter, we will look at the IRS in detail to understand what it stands for and what their real business pertains to.

The internal revenue system is chiefly responsible for collecting taxes in the United States. The IRS was set up in 1862 by President Abraham Lincoln and now operates under the direction of the United States Department of Treasury.

The IRS collects taxes from the public such as income tax, corporate tax, estate or property tax, gift etc. All of these are levied on employed personnel or businesses.

The IRS finds its headquarters in Washington, DC. The government body has its work cut out, as there are millions of people who file for tax returns and also millions of companies that do the same.

Around ten years ago, the IRS claimed to have earned trillions of dollars through 133 million taxpayers and 6 million corporate companies. This sum has only grown in value over the years and will continue to grow for a long time.

If you are a taxpayer, then you have to remain in the good books of the IRS. After all, you want your business to run smoothly for many years without any unnecessary glitches.

First off, do not ignore any notices that you have received from the IRS. These notices are meant to remind you about something that needs to be done. If you showcase a *no-cares* attitude towards it then you are sure to get into trouble. Instead, you must keep track of all the notices and reminders that you have received and take action. Most of the time, the IRS sends an official letter only when it wishes to correct something, like correcting an amount that is to be collected from you. So, going through the sent letter will only benefit your company. You can get your secretary to attach high authority to any letter that you receive from the IRS.

You have to go through your taxpayers' account from time to time to check if everything is fine. Checking to see if there are any dues or fines or whether the IRS has prepared your tax filing etc. will go a long way in helping you remain on top of your game. You can take away a lot of stress just by being proactive.

Sometimes, discrepancies might occur between you and the IRS, and you might have to stand up to them. Here is what you can do in such a situation.

Standing up to the IRS

Many times, people end up employing the wrong person to prepare their taxes. This can lead to a harrowing experience, as it is important to find the right person to file taxes for your company. However, if you unfortunately have ended up with the wrong preparer then you have to be wise about it. Don't make the mistake of being unprofessional, as it will look bad. Instead, inform the IRS about the situation and tell them that you chose the wrong person to file your taxes. They might understand and give you grace time to fix any issues. The next logical move would be for you to find a better person to file your tax.

Remember to never get into frivolous arguments with the IRS agent. They are generally very smart and will know to show you your place in no time at all! You have to remember to always make a logical point and then argue on the basis of it. If you plan on picking a point that isn't too strong and base an argument on it then you will lose focus in no time. If you are not sure what to say or how to respond, then either remain quiet or take the help of your accountant.

It would be a very serious mistake to offer a bribe to an IRS agent. There is no point in trying to bribe someone, especially when they are extremely powerful. There have been several instances of people being jailed for offering bribes to an agent. Don't think you can offer a meaty sum and they will oblige. You might have to go to prison for it.

Don't blindly trust the IRS when they say you owe them money. You have to cross check to see if you really do. It pays to know in advance if you have to disburse money to someone and the best thing is to maintain a journal to record it. If it matches your records, then you can be sure about it. If no such entry exists in your record, then obviously you don't owe them money.

You have to be prepared for an audit well in advance. Many companies make the mistake of not preparing for one and when the auditor shows up at the door, run to hide their records. Doing so will make it extremely suspicious and the auditor might decide to fine you for such behavior. Remain ready for an audit at all times to avoid rushing at the last minute.

It is believed that the IRS is working towards reducing the burden that small companies have to bear with, in terms of paying taxes. It would be helpful for the many companies to pay less, especially if they are unable to come up with the requisite profits.

These form the different ways in which you can remain in the good books of the IRS.

Chapter 4

Taxes and Your Business

In this chapter, we will individually look at the taxation laws that apply to sole proprietors, LLCs and startups.

Sole proprietor

Definition: a sole proprietor is one who single handedly owns and operates a business. The person is a single owner of the business and is responsible for its running and debts. The proprietor can have a helping hand but will remain the sole owner of the company.

The sole proprietor can operate the business under his own name or pick a fictitious one.

The sole proprietor will independently fund the business with his own money. In case he is unable to do so, then he can borrow money from creditors. In case he is unable to pay them back through his business profits, then creditors can sue him and seek compensation through the sale of personal belongings.

Sole proprietors often mix their personal earnings and that of their business and prefer to own just a single account. It helps the proprietor keep track of expenses and incomes.

Tax laws for sole proprietor

The taxation laws for sole proprietors are pretty easy to understand. Since they will single handedly run the business, any income that the business makes will count as the individual's income. The same income is taxable.

The sole proprietor has to declare his income (profit/loss) from business by filling the out a Schedule C along with a standard form 1040. This is the only difference that there is between a sole proprietor and an individual filing income tax.

One great aspect of this form is that you can have the bottom line amount from the business transferred to your personal account. You can offset your losses with any profit that you make through other sources.

A sole proprietor must additionally file a Schedule SE with Form 1040. The SE stands for self-employment and you have to calculate the self-employment tax that you have to pay to the government.

There are many advantages to being a sole proprietor. The owner can avoid paying unemployment tax. Since the owner can mix personal and company assets, it becomes quite easy for him to bail out of debts.

LLC

Definition: A limited liability company is one where the members of the company cannot be held liable for the debts of the company. The liability of the members is limited which means that they do not have to shell out personal effects to repay any company debts.

The IRS does not have any specific LLC tax rules. If there is more than one owner of the LLC, then the IRS treats it as a partnership firm. If there is a single owner, then you can file taxes as a sole proprietor.

If you wish to treat your LLC as a corporate company, then you have to pay corporate tax.

If you wish to treat your company as a partnership, then you have to fill out Form 1065. The IRS does not require you to pay any taxes on your business earnings. Any information in regards to profits and losses is declared by the individual owners.

The LLC has to report every individual holder's share on a Schedule K-1 form at the end of the financial year. This means the LLC will cause the individual's income to be doubly taxed.

The corporate business entity will be solely responsible for declaring all incomes on Form 1120.

Remember that failing to file for taxes through the LLC does not make the owners personally liable.

However, the owners have to undertake double taxation. They will first be taxed as a corporate and secondly, the owners will be taxed for the dividends that they receive.

As for sole proprietors, we already looked at the requirements for filing taxes, in the previous segment.

Startup

Definition: Startup companies are entrepreneurial ventures of new businesses. It can be a company, a partnership or a business organization that someone starts as a small business.

Start-ups are generally viewed as companies that hope to grow into something big over a specific period of time. But at the beginning, the owners remain unassuming of the company's true potential.

The taxation laws for start-ups are pretty straightforward. You will have to fill out Form 1065, just like a partnership firm would.

But if you are calling it a corporation then you can fill out Form 1120.

These form the various taxation rules for the different types of companies. It is best to prepare for filing well in advance to avoid a last minute rush.

Chapter 5
Choosing the Right Business Type

Whether you acquired an existing business or are going to start a brand new organization, you should first choose which type of organization (or "business entity") is best for you. There are a few business approaches, and each has strengths and weaknesses. Ensure that you consult with your lawyer or accountant about which sort of business is most suitable for your specific circumstance before settling on a definite conclusion.

Why Pick a C Corporation?

While selecting an organization, the C Corporation, or C-Corp, is the most widely recognized Corporation type, it isn't, however, the top choice for most small business owners. C Corporations give constrained risk security to proprietors, who are called shareholders, which means proprietors are normally not taxed on business obligations and liabilities. Beginning a C Corporation may likewise offer more prominent tax points of interest due to an extended capacity to deduct worker advantages, which are regularly utilized by developing organizations.

C Corp Favorable Circumstances

Beginning a C Corporation commonly gives various points of interest:

Limited risk assurance

Proprietors are not commonly taxed on business obligations and liabilities.

Unlimited proprietors

C Corps can have a boundless number of shareholders.

Easy exchange of proprietorship

A proprietorship is effortlessly transferable through the offer of stock.

Unlimited life

At the point when a C Corporation's proprietor acquires an impairing sickness or dies, the Corporation does not stop to exist.

The proprietors take sensible pay rates

Pay rates paid to the proprietors of a C Corporation are assessed to them as payment for work done and they are deducted from the C Corp benefits for money tax purposes.

Owners aren't accordingly taxed on business profit

As opposed to going through entities like LLCs, the income of a C Corporation is not automatically taxed to the proprietors. They are taxed to the proprietors if profits have been appropriated to them. The C Corp pays tax on its salary at C Corp tax rates.

Raise capital effortlessly

Extra capital can be raised by offering shares of stock.

Preserve income inside the business

A C Corp could effectively hold income for reasonable business needs, in the event that it consents to the collected profit and tax procurements, rather than appropriating them to shareholders.

Integrity

C Corps might be seen as a more expert/authentic element than a sole proprietorship or general partnership.

Lower audit peril

For the most part, C Corporations are inspected less than sole proprietorships and then only every now and again.

Tax deductible costs

Costs of doing business might be tax deductible.

Self-employment tax savings

Actually, C Corporation can tender self-employment tax savings as proprietors who work for the business are delegated representatives.

C Corp Key Benefits

C Corporations are more adaptable than S Corporations as far as the quantity of proprietors (shareholders) they can have and who can be a proprietor. That is one motivation behind why C Corps are the go-to business type for financial speculators when they give subsidies to a business.

Bear in Mind

Companies confront the broadest progressive taxes of any business type. C Corporations should embrace and consistently overhaul standing rules, hold and legitimately archive yearly gatherings of executives and shareholders, and that's only the tip of the iceberg.

Why Pick an S Corporation?

S Corps are Corporations that have chosen a unique tax status with the IRS. S Corporations give the same constrained obligation to the proprietors (called shareholders) as C Corporations, implying that proprietors regularly are not generally taxable on business debts and obligations; in any case, S Corporations have gone through taxes. S Corps do not pay tax at the business level, but they document an informational tax return. This gathered information about business income / loss is then accounted for in the proprietors' personal tax returns, and any tax due is remunerated at the individual level.

S Corp favorable benefits

Forming an S Corporation has numerous favorable benefits. Various small business owners form a Corporation and choose an S-Corp status in order to go through taxation. There are a wide variety of points of interest of developing an S Corporation which include the following:

Limited risk security

Proprietors are not normally taxed on S Corporation business debts and obligations.

Easy exchange of proprietorship

A proprietorship is effortlessly transferable through the offer of stock.

Unlimited life

At the point when an S Corporation's proprietor becomes the victim of a crippling sickness or dies, the Corporation does not stop to exist.

Go through taxation in the Corporate form

S Corporation tax status evades the "double-taxation" connected with C-Corps and rather furnishes S Corp proprietors with go through tax advantages.

Raise capital effectively

Extra capital can be raised by offering shares of stock.

Integrity

S Corps might be seen as a more expert/true entity than a sole proprietorship or general partnership. We will discuss more about sole proprietorship vs. S Corp later.

Pro-rata dissemination of benefits

Under the IRS S Corp tax system, benefits, losses and other go through things are dispensed in view of every shareholder's proportionate share of stock.

Income & losses conceded to shareholders

Wages and losses of S Corps have gone through to shareholders, like the way salary and losses of organizations go through to partners.

Lower audit peril

For the most part, S Corps are inspected less often than sole proprietorships.

Tax deductible costs

Costs of doing business might be tax deductible.

Self- employment tax savings

S Corp can offer self-employment tax savings since proprietors who work for the business are delegated representatives.

S Corp organization proprietorship confinements

Per IRS rules, S Corp organization proprietors (shareholders) must meet the following criteria:

- Only 100 or less at one given time.

- Must be US nationals/inhabitants (can't be non-occupant outsiders).
- Can't be C enterprises, different S organizations, (LLCs) limited liability companies, partnerships, or other certain trusts.

Different IRS limitations, aside from proprietorship confinements, likewise apply to S partnerships. For instance, there can be one and only one class of stock (which contrasts with voting rights that are passable) and the partnership must be a resident company.

Key Benefits of an S Enterprise

Choosing an S enterprise status with the IRS takes into consideration that it will go through taxation of the company's benefits. S corps should, in any case, file corporate tax returns, yet they don't disburse tax at the corporate level. The S company's benefits have gone through to the individual tax returns of the shareholders, and taxes are paid on those benefits at the individual tax rate.

Remember

S companies should make a filing of Form 2553 with the IRS. The form should be finished and documented at any time prior to the sixteenth day of the third month of the taxable year in which the election is to produce results, or at whatever time during the tax year that precedes the tax year in which it is to produce results.

A correlation between S Corporations and C Corporations

At the point when you are beginning a new business or changing your business structure, one of the most important factors among the well-known alternatives that small business owners have is to assess whether to form an (S Corp) S Corporation or (C Corp) C Corporation. These are the two most basic approaches to join on the web, and the decision truly relies on your business objectives.

The Similarities

The C Corporation is the customary Corporation whilst the S Corporation has chosen an uncommon tax status with the IRS. It gets its name since it is characterized in Subchapter S of the Internal Revenue Code. To choose S Corporation status while developing a Corporation, Form 2553 should be documented with the IRS and all S Corporation rules must be met. Be that as it may, C Corporations and S Corporations share numerous qualities:

- *Limited risk insurance*

Both offer restricted risk security, so shareholders (proprietors) are ordinarily not generally at risk for taxation of business debts and obligations.

- *Distinct entities*

Both the S Corp and C Corp are distinct lawful entities made by a state filing.

- *Filing archives*

Development documents should be filed by the state. These reports, normally called the Articles of Incorporation or else Certificate of Incorporation, are similar in both C and S Corporations.

- *Structure*

Both have shareholders, executives, and officers. Shareholders are the proprietors of the organization and choose the governing body, who then supervise and coordinate Corporation dealings and basic leadership, yet are not taxed on everyday operations. The executives choose officers to oversee day by day business undertakings.

- *Corporate customs*

Both are required to take after the same inward and outward corporate customs and commitments, for example embracing standing rules, issuing stock, holding shareholder and director meetings, filing yearly reports, and paying yearly taxes.

The contrasts

In spite of their numerous similarities, S Corporations and C Corporations also have quite a few differences.

- *Taxation*

The tax is regularly viewed as the most noteworthy contrast for small entrepreneurs while assessing S Corporations versus C Corporations.

C Corporations. C Corps are independently taxable entities. They document a corporate government (Form 1120) and pay taxes at the corporate level. They likewise may fall under double taxation if corporate salary is appropriated to entrepreneurs as profits, which are viewed as individual pay. Tax on Corporate wage is paid first at the Corporate level and again at the individual level of profits.

S Corporations. S-Corps are go through tax entities. They document an informational federal return (Form the 1120s). However, no income tax is paid at the corporate level. The benefits/losses of the business are "passed through" the business, and they are accounted for on the proprietors' personal tax returns. Whatever tax is due is paid at the individual level through the proprietors.

Personal Income Taxes. With both types of corporations, personal income tax is also due on any pay drawn from the corporation and from any profits received from the Corporation.

- *Corporate possession*

C Corporations have no confinements on proprietorship, however, S Corporations do. S Corps are confined to a maximum of 100 shareholders, and shareholders should be US taxpayers/inhabitants. S Corporations cannot be claimed by C Corporations, various S Corporations, LLCs, partnerships or a variety of trusts.

Additionally, S Corporations can have one and only one class of stock (ignoring voting rights), while C Corporations can have different classes. C Corporations accordingly provide more adaptability when beginning a business in the event that you plan to develop and extend the possession or offer your Corporation for sale.

S Corporation decision

To develop into an S Corporation, you should file Form 2553 with the IRS. The IRS guidelines — which can be somewhat hard to understand — require that an election is viewed as completed in the present tax year, which is done if the Form 2553 is finished and filed in the following manner:

- Any time before the sixteenth day of the third month (for calendar year taxpayers, this implies it needs to happen by March fifteenth).
- Any time during the previous tax year (notwithstanding that an election made no later than 2 months and 15 days after the start of a tax year that is under 2½ months in length is dealt with as auspicious for that year).

For the most part, an election made after the fifteenth day of the third month but before the end of the tax year is viable for the following tax year (unless you can demonstrate an inability to file on time through a sensible cause). Remember that a few states additionally require you to document a state-level S Corporation election in the wake of joining your business.

Limited Liability Company (LLC)

To begin with, there are no tax preferences (or drawbacks) to shaping an LLC. Actually, shaping an LLC won't modify anything for federal income tax purposes. Single-proprietor LLCs are taxed simply like sole proprietorships, and various proprietor LLCs are taxed simply like partnerships.

You ought to, nonetheless, know that developing an LLC may subject your business to extra state taxes. Certain states (California, for example) subject LLCs to "franchise taxes" notwithstanding a run of the standard income tax.

Sole Proprietorships & Partnerships

In general, there isn't anything wrong with working your business as a sole proprietorship or partnership, but you should know that you will have a bigger risk for business debts. As it were, if your business is sued for any reason, the offended party may have the capacity to come after your own personal assets, and not only the assets of the business.

Various Key Points

- If you don't plan to dole out the greater part of the benefits from your business, you may profit by shaping a C-Corp and using a technique recognized as "income splitting." The thought is to part the business pay so that a part of it is taxable to the enterprise and part of it is taxable to the company's owner(s), in this manner putting them each in a lower tax bracket than they would be in if only one entity was winning the majority of the income.

- The huge disadvantage to C-Corp taxation is that the circulations of benefits (identified as "dividends") are liable to double taxation. At the end of the day, the organization is taxed once on its pay, and after that, the shareholders are taxed on any profits they get as well.

Also, similar to S-companies, C-enterprises are more legally bound from a bookkeeping, tax, and legitimacy viewpoint than sole proprietorships, partnerships, or LLCs. All things considered, C-Corp proprietors have a tendency to bring about fairly high legal and bookkeeping costs.

Tax & Business Formations

Exactly how are the reimbursements of the different structures is taxed?

- A sole merchant utilizes their individual tax identification number, incorporates wages from the business in their return, and pays tax on that wage and any other pay earned, for example pay, wages, and investment income.

- A partnership has a different partnership tax identification number and files a partnership tax return to show points of interest on business revenue and costs. However, it does not pay tax. With a partnership, the tax return demonstrates who is responsible for what portion of the organization's profits and losses. Every partner must declare their portion of the partner's profit or loss on their individual tax forms.

A trust handles revenue in a similar fashion to a partnership. The difference is that a trust never has to allocate its losses. It must have a different trust tax document number, and the trust tax return demonstrates points of interest to pay and costs. In general, where the entire amount of the trust wage is allocated to an adult resident recipient, the trust is not obligated to pay taxes. A trust more often than not circulates benefits to recipients, who then demonstrate their portion of trust salary on their personal tax returns.

A firm has its own specific tax identification number as well as tax return and pays tax at the organization tax. Forming your business will have tax, reporting, and compliance requirements for both you and your business.

Chapter 6

Tax Saving Strategies for Small Businesses

Companies have the chance to reduce the amount of taxes that they have to pay towards the IRS. In this chapter, we will look at the different things that you can do to reduce how much tax you pay.

Choose the right type of business

First off, start by picking the right term to fit your business into. That is, be sure whether you want to be a sole proprietor or an LLC. You have to pick the right one in order to pay the right tax. Don't be under the impression that you can choose whatever you think sounds good. You have to pick something that will help you avail tax benefits. For example, a sole proprietor can take advantage of many deductions while filing for taxes whereas members of an

LLC will not be held personally liable to any debts that the company owes.

Work opportunity tax credit

Work opportunity tax credit refers to a tax deduction that you can avail for hiring a war veteran or someone that has faced significant difficulties in finding a job to suit their cadre. You can show the IRS their employment letter and also the salary that you pay them. The amount paid will be deducted from your tax. There is a limit to how many you can employ or use as a means to reduce your company's tax.

Retirement benefits

You can offer retirement benefits to your employees which will help you save on taxes. You must choose the best plans that suit your business. Retirement benefits can range from providing a monthly pension to paying monthly bills that your employees might incur after they retire. So, you have to choose the best plans and help save on a large amount of taxes that you might have to pay to the IRS.

Unify

If you have a slew of companies, then you can consider bringing all of them under a single roof, as that will help you pay a unique tax. You don't have to worry about filing different papers for each individual company. You can file for just one and be done with it in no time at all. You can in fact, offset the losses of a company with the profits of another. You can also increase the number of deductions that you make. Doing so will greatly help you remain with a large profit at the end and might not have to pay up as many taxes.

Independent contractors

There is an advantage to employing independent contractors as opposed to employees. If you are running a business or company, then you can consider employing independent contractors, as they will help you avoid paying payroll taxes. This is great for all those small business that are looking to capitalize on small profits. You can also employ freelancers if you like.

Hiring family

It is a good idea for you to employ your children and family members to work for you. Doing so will help you avoid paying them an allowance and you can deduct their salaries from your tax returns. It need not always be your kith and kin and can be cousins, aunts, uncles etc. This is especially beneficial for sole proprietors. They will not owe any social security or Medicare taxes on their children's salaries, which will prove to be quite advantageous.

Write off assets twice

Better known as a gift lease back, you can write off an asset like a vehicle twice. Like a vehicle that you use for your business, which is fully depreciated. Its market value stands at $15,000. You decide to lease it out to your spouse for $500 a month. You can then avail a benefit of $6,000, which can be deducted from your taxation.

Travel/ medical expenses

You can take advantage of travel and medical expenses reimbursements. And it is not just yours that you can reimburse, you can reimburse your business partner's, spouses, children's, dependent's etc. You can produce appropriate receipts and avail the deductions. We will look at the different receipts that you can produce in a future chapter of this book.

Renting your house

If you own a house, then you can rent it out to an S corporation and earn tax-free income from it. You can rent it out to a company for about 14 days a month to conduct meetings and seminars etc. and not declare it. But remember there is a limit to how many people can occupy it at any given point in time. Also, you have to specify to the company that there can be no entertainment provided during the meetings. If you own an S corporation then you can use your house for meetings and deduct rent to yourself from company accounts.

Telephone/ Internet bills

It is a common practice among sole proprietors to use their phone for professional and personal uses and then deduct the phone bill from their business taxes.   You can also maintain two different phones if you like and use the bills to avail a relief. The same extends to any stationery and other things that you buy for your company on a regular basis.

These form the different things that you can do to reduce the amount of taxes that you pay to the IRS.

Secure Tax Scheduling For High-Net-Worth

Generally, when affluent people must discuss their tax practices and arrangements, they do it in quiet tones — looking over their shoulders as though trying to save all the money they can is somehow swindling the legislature. In reality, however, the IRS has no inclination toward any one taxpayer, and pays little heed to high salaried individuals or corporations that take advantage of favorable circumstances of lawful techniques for tax minimization. Sadly, the well off have a number of the most widely recognized tax breaks eliminated because of their high salary levels. That doesn't mean legitimate tax minimization opportunities don't exist for the rich. With a little learning, imagination, and forward thinking, individuals and corporations in a higher tax bracket can save more on their taxes than the average American makes every year.

Lawful Tactics for Shielding Employment Income

In his enlightening book, "The Millionaire Next Door" (1996), Thomas Stanley exposed that at the time 66% of moguls in the U.S. were independently employed or were small entrepreneurs. Significantly more individuals work for outside organizations and run a small home business more as an afterthought. For those small entrepreneurs, there are huge tax break opportunities that are not subject to the standard pay constraints.

Maybe one of the best tax decrease opportunities is the utilization of small business retirement procedures. Under current laws, the IRS normally does exclude cash added to these plans in the benefits of an entrepreneur or independently employed the person. On the off chance that a rich taxpayer can defer over the top spending until retirement, tax collection on those supports can be delayed. Remember, though, that if you do not pay taxes on your retirement savings now, you will have to pay taxes on it later when it is withdrawn.

Protecting salary through augmenting the operation of the small business with healthcare and employee benefit procedures is another option. By setting up health investment accounts, wellbeing reimbursement options, and Section 125 plans, costs that would have been over the reasoning limits for individual taxpayers can be paid on a pretax premise through the business as a simple business expense.

Another legitimate pay shielding method is to put posterity in the finance of a business. Doing this provides you with two noteworthy advantages: FICA and federal unemployment taxes should not have to be paid if the child is a minor, and the child might have the capacity to add to an IRA out of earned wages. Utilizing a spouse gathers comparative results. Since there is a yearly cap on the amount of FICA that an individual should pay, one life partner can be remunerated considerably higher than the point of confinement. Doing this may imply that one life partner pays less into the Social Security framework, yet it additionally gives a couple the chance to invest privately as opposed to placing it in the hands of the Social Security framework.

Methods for Sheltering Investment Income

The Roth IRA is among the best tax break options, which makes it possible to delay tax payment for decades. Tragically, numerous prosperous speculators are not allowed to utilize them in light of the fact that their net gross wages are too high. These investors can think about subsidizing as a non-deductible Traditional IRA. While these IRAs don't give immediate payout or tax-free withdrawals, the profit can aggregate now on a tax-deferred premise over a long period of time.

Another underutilized tax reduction procedure is "tax lot matching." This practice licenses an investor to specify which shares of a stock or common subsidies he or she is offering, rather than the default IRS technique of (FIFO) first in, first out. Tax lot matching can give tremendous payback when shares of a stock that show little pickup or even a loss are sold, rather than selling shares from long-haul ventures that show significant picks up. Well-off investors with children have even more opportunities to shelter venture pay and pick-ups from the IRS.

A standout among the most prominent options is the (UTMA) uniform transfer of gifts to minor's custodial accounts, which has dropped out of the spotlight subsequent to the presentation of 529 plans. While these accounts may never again be the best school investment fund vehicles, they offer an interesting open door. A parent who possesses exceedingly valuable shares of stock can "gift" the stock to a youth and then have the child tender it and report a part of the benefits of the child's generously lower tax bracket later. Prosperous parents and grandparents have the new option of utilizing Section 529 plans to move cash out of their bequests, and shield the development of significant sums of the future income taxes, if they are being utilized for the school costs of any relative.

Under the Internal Revenue Code, any benefactor can gift up to five times their yearly gift barring restraint into a Section 529 account for a child, and the length of the various donations for the identical individual isn't specified in the five-year take-over time frame. With the top bequest tax section surpassing half, this can level with an estate tax investment fund of more than $25,000 for each $50,000 gift. In summary, wealthy investors who have altruistic

ies ought to abstain from giving money however could be expected.

The IRS permits investors to give considerably refreshing securities to not-for-profit firms and take a discount for everything. This spares investors the inconvenience of selling the advantages themselves, paying tax on the pickup and give slighter gifts to the philanthropy. To put it plainly, give the stock and keep the money.

Advanced Tax Strategy to Avoid State Income Taxes

While corporate tax reversals have gotten all the press recently, there is an additional tax procedure — described as a "personal tax inversion" — that can facilitate minimizing our taxes. Be that as it may, like corporate tax reversals, the individual form is turning out to be just as disputable. Prior to this year, New York state, which was losing an estimated $150 million a year through tax evasion, successfully shut this tax loophole for New York inhabitants. Different states may follow suit, but until then, on the off chance that you anticipate a fortune from a one-time raise or else an investment account that you suspect to deliver noteworthy income over the coming years, a personal tax reversal may be a good option.

The personal tax reversal procedure is not ideal for every situation, but under the right circumstances it can be a compelling approach to pay less state income tax. The procedure, which works best on the off chance that you reside in a state with a high income tax, necessitates the utilization of an Incomplete Non-Grantor Trust. The Incomplete Non-Grantor Trust permits you to move advantages to another state with a lower or no state income tax, for example to Nevada or Delaware.

These structures are likewise alluded to as NINGs or DINGs to mirror the state (Nevada and Delaware, individually) in which the trust is found. The NING makes it possible for certain persons with huge speculation pay to decrease their aggregate tax cost by keeping away from all state income taxes that may be levied in some way or another.

Just How Does a NING/DING Mechanism Work?

There are grantor trusts as well as non-grantor trusts. A grantor trust is set up by an individual called the grantor. With a grantor trust, the grantor (explicitly, you) is dealt with as owning the trust resources for income tax intentions, and all things considered, is taxable on any income tax due on the advantages inside of the trust. For instance, in the event that you live in California and have a trust controlled in Nevada, you will, in any case, be taxed as a California occupant.

On the other hand, a non-grantor trust is the place you put resources into the trust and surrender enough tax strings so you are no longer considered the "proprietor" for tax purposes. So now the trust itself is responsible for paying the income tax and not you. On the off chance that the trust is controlled by a tax-free state, for example, Nevada, the trust pays no state tax, but don't celebrate too early. On the off chance that you exchange capital outside of your jurisdiction, you may fall under the classification of paying gift taxes. So while you may keep away from the state income tax, you would in all likelihood need to pay federal gift tax if nothing else goes through your gift and/or home tax deduction if your lawyer is not cautious when drafting your returns. A non-grantor trust isn't going to function admirably if this were somehow to happen.

The most common arrangement is to utilize a NING or DING. The secret ingredient for this formation is the vigilant drafting of the reports. The objective is to retain enough control of the trust so that you are not blamed for gifting the profits and paying gift tax, while at the same time not retaining so much control that you are taxable by state income tax. This is a propelled system that requires the direction of a decent estate or tax lawyer. Nevada has turned into the go-to state for this procedure. Individuals love to not have to pay state income tax.

An additional advantage is that NINGs and DINGs give tax minimization opportunities as well as resource assurance. In the off chance that you are levied with minimizing state income taxes, have your counselors run an investigation to check whether a (NING) Nevada Incomplete Non-Grantor Trust or a (DING) Delaware Incomplete Non-Grantor Trust will work for you.

Sketchy Strategies to Avoid

As specified previously, the IRS has no issue with well-off investors keeping away from as much tax as legally acceptable. Still, no article about wealthy tax arranging methods would be complete without a caution about the practices that can get you in trouble with the IRS. Despite the fact that you may catch individuals boasting about these procedures at mixed drinks gatherings, be admonished — they can prompt fines and even jail time.

The most mainstream of the damaging tax techniques that receive an overwhelming amount of IRS trials is holding offshore asset trusts. While it might sound exceptionally high class to have a Swiss or Cayman Islands financial account, these accounts are illegal when used to maintain a strategic distance from U.S. income taxes. Moreover, the different post-9/11 regulations put strict points of confinement on the amount of cash that can be lawfully exchanged offshore and for what purposes this cash is being used. In the event that somebody prescribes that you utilize one of these trusts, you should get second and third opinions from other independent tax professionals.

The IRS additionally disapproves of rich investors directing interactions that are not at arm's length to equivocate tax. To put it plainly, all exchanges among related gatherings ought to be led as though they were made between two totally alien parties. For instance, the parents who offer their land to their children for half of the market value (to abstain from paying tax on the income) would not likely do this with a total stranger. Prosperous tax methodologies that are not done in an arm's-length fashion are liable to draw IRS scrutiny.

Ultimately, (FLP) family limited partnerships have turned into a mainstream method for endeavoring to exchange advantages for the cutting edge, with the method of parents both holding control of the benefits and keeping away from gift tax rules being the most common. While there are examples where such associations can be appropriately organized, they are manhandled enough to accumulate overwhelming examination from the IRS. Utilizing an FLP will probably place you and the greater part of your other tax procedures under the IRS magnifying glass.

A Few Tax Guidelines for Small Organizations

Just because tax law can be intricate doesn't mean that you need to be overwhelmed. There are a handful of tips on the best means to cope with your taxes year-round.

Consider Taxes Throughout the Entire Year

Small entrepreneurs ought not to regard taxes as a once-a-year occasion. Rather, tax arrangements ought to be a year-round activity. Procrastinating until the very last minute makes tax readiness more convoluted, and it constrains your cash sparing choices by rushing you through the process.

Get Professional Help

Specialists will tell you that a proficient tax lawyer or bookkeeper is certainly justified regardless of the cost. Tax laws can be mind boggling, and they are difficult for some bustling small entrepreneurs to figure out. An expert can easily identify tax reductions and breaks that you would otherwise miss.

Be Conscientious

Indeed, a small business owner must stay aware of news identified with the tax laws. Pay particular attention to business news and also stay alert of Congress' work on tax laws.

File on time!

Lastly, remember to always file your taxes on time. It is the most basic thing that you can do to avoid paying more. There is no point in inviting unwanted fines. If you want to file late because of unavoidable circumstances, then notify the IRS in advance so that they know you will be paying your taxes late. Don't expect them to understand, as they will quickly issue you a fine without waiting for a reply from you. We looked at the different ways in which you can buy time to pay your taxes and you can go through it once again to understand it better.

Chapter 7

Employing a Professional Tax Preparer

Paying taxes can seem like a herculean task to someone who is doing it for the first time. In fact, those that pay regularly will also feel like it is a demanding task where one wrong move can land you in trouble.

But don't worry; you can enlist the help of a professional tax preparer to help you prepare your taxes. Professional taxpayers can be chartered accountants or a qualified tax preparer.

Here are some aspects you must bear in mind while hiring a tax preparer.

No one size fits all

Before you start hunting for the best tax preparer, you have to understand that there will not be a standard agent who will come over and prepare your taxes. So stop asking your family and friends to suggest you the best one, as you will have to do the dirty work yourself. You have to put in efforts to find the one that will best suit your business. Start early, so that you can spend some time looking for the best person to file your taxes.

Look for PTIN

The next thing is to check whether the person has a valid preparer tax identification number. Better known as PTIN, this is a number that tells you whether the person is a qualified preparer or not. Do make it a point to ask this at the very beginning as you don't want to end up with someone who does not have the number and has yet prepared your tax papers for you.

Qualifications

The next thing is to check the qualifications of the person. Most tax preparers like to add in many alphabets next to their name to showcase their qualifications. But just a bunch of letters next to each other does not mean they are highly qualified. It can just mean they have passed a few necessary tests. It is ideal for the person to have a CFP qualification that stands for certified financial planner board of planners. You can also see if the person is a qualified lawyer with a JD or LLM.

History

Next, you have to check the tax preparer's history. You have to see if they have prepared tax forms in the past. You can ask them for a background check and see who they have worked with. You can also visit their website (if they have one) and look up testimonials. It is important for you to do your research before hiring someone, as you cannot take your taxes lightly.

How well versed?

The next thing to check is how well versed the person is with the state and city rules. Any professional tax preparer will be well versed in federal tax rules since it is universal. But, the state and city rules differ between states, which make it important for the preparer to know about them well in advance. You can ask and find out if he knows about the rules.

Providing forms

When you wish to prepare the taxes then you obviously have to provide the right documents for the taxes. You have to provide the tax preparer with Forms W-2, 1099 and

1098. These forms will contain information with regard to your incomes and expenses. You must also be ready to provide the preparer with any other information that he or she seeks. Preparing everything in advance will help you remain ready at the last minute.

Fees

Many first time tax preparer employers make the mistake of not asking how much the fees will be. In fact, that is not even the right approach to take while asking about the fees. You have to ask how the fees will be determined and on what basis you are being charged whatever you are. Fees are extremely important to settle well in advance to avoid any discrepancies later. Before you have the final word, you have to have a specific number in mind to know if you are paying the right amount. It is vital to avoid those preparers that ask you for a percentage of what you will be filing. Whether you file a large sum or a small one, you have to ultimately pay the preparer his rightful due and not any more.

Electronic filing

Remember to settle for a preparer that is well versed in electronic filing. After all, you want someone that will do his job quickly and help you finish up with all legal processes at the earliest. It is quite simple to file electronically and you can save on a lot of time and effort. If you are well versed with it but your preparer isn't, then you can assist him while he files electronically.

Audits

Next, you must ask your tax preparer if he will be ready for an audit. Everybody dreads an audit for obvious reasons, but it is best to prepare for one in advance in order to avoid issues later. If your tax preparer has faced an audit before then well and good, but if he has not, then you must ask him how you can prepare for one in advance.

Contact

You must ensure that the tax preparer is easily reachable and you can give him a call at any time of the day. It is best to ask for multiple contact details so that you can at least pursue one of them to successfully contact him.

Return copy

You have to ask your tax preparer for a copy of the tax return that was filed for you. It might take some time for the preparer to file all the papers and assemble them in the correct order, but you must ensure that you get a copy before he files it. You have to go through all the details to see if everything is fine.

Signature

It is extremely important for a tax preparer to sign the tax document. If your filed paper is not carrying a valid signature then you might be in a sticky spot. If your tax preparer is not willingly signing, then you should get him to at any cost. In fact, you might want to reconsider him if he is putting up a fight.

Advantages of filing it yourself

There are certain advantages of filing taxes by yourself. First off, nobody knows your company better than yourself, so, you will be able to file taxes best. You can start filing early and be done with it on time.

Even if it seems like a herculean task, doing it once will give you the confidence to do it every year. It will get progressively easier for you.

You can save on the fees that you have to pay the tax preparer. Most tax preparers charge a hefty sum, which will turn out to be an additional and unnecessary expense.

There are not many deductions to make you can easily file your own taxes. Many times, people don't understand what needs to be deducted from where and why. They end up forgetting something and wonder what went wrong. So, if you don't have properties, investments and other such deductions to make then you can prepare the taxes by yourself.

But remember that you have to do it by yourself if you know the basic rules and regulations of taxation. If you have been paying income tax then you will be well versed with the procedure. But if you are doing it for the first time then you will have to seek professional help.

Final word: It is better to have a professional prepare your taxes for you as that can help take a lot of load off your shoulders. Many taxpayers worry about filing their taxes and end up making mistakes. As you know, it is extremely important not to make any mistake while filing taxes and you have to be quite careful with it. If you are filing for the first time, then you must compulsorily avail help lest you end up making unnecessary mistakes.

Chapter 8

Company Tax Payers Check List

In this chapter we will look at the company taxpayer's checklist to make it easy for you to file your taxes.

Incomes

- All gross receipts derived from sales and services
- All sales records
- All returns and allowances
- Business checking account interest accrued
- Business savings account interest accrued
- Any other incomes

Expenses incurred for sold goods (if any)

- All Inventory information
- Beginning inventory total sum in dollars
- Inventory purchases made during the year
- Ending inventory total sum in dollars

- Any personal use items
- All raw materials and supplies purchased

Overall expenses accrued by the company

- Advertising costs incurred
- Telephone and cellphone bills accrued
- Internet and computer charges incurred
- Any travel and transportation charges incurred/ receipts
- Local transportation charges/ receipts
- Any Business trip charges/ receipts
- All tolls and or parking receipts paid/ receipts
- Any personal travels charges/ receipts
- Any airplane charges/ receipts
- Any hotel room charges/ receipts
- Any meals charges
- Any taxi charges
- Any Internet connection charges
- Any Other charges
- Any Commissions paid to subcontractors
- File Form 1099-MISC and 1096 as necessary
- Any depreciation
- Any Cost of business assets
- Any cost of personal assets
- Any disposition date of used assets sold

- Any Business insurance
- Any Casualty loss insurance
- Any Errors and omissions
- Any Other expenses
- Any Mortgage interest on building owned by business
- Any Business loan interest accrued
- Any Investment expense and interest accrued
- Any Professional fees accrued
- Any Lawyers, accountants, and consultant's charges accrued
- Any Office supplies purchased
- Any stationary such as Pens, paper, staples, and other consumables
- Any other Rent expense accrued
- Any Office space rent accrued
- Any Business-use vehicle lease expense accrued
- Any Other expenses
- Any Office-in-home
- Any Square footage of office space used
- Any Total square footage of home used
- Any Hours of home daycare provided
- Any Mortgage interest or rent paid
- Any Homeowner's or renters' insurance amount

- Any Utilities purchased
- Any Cost of home, separate improvements and first date of business use
- Any Wages paid to employees
- Fill out Form W-2 and W-3
- Any Federal and state payroll returns i.e. Form 940, Form 941, etc.
- Any Employee benefit expenses
- Payment to Contractors
- Fill out Form 1099-MISc
- Fill out Form 1096
- Any Other expenses accrued
- Any Repairs, maintenance of office facility, etc.
- Any Estimated tax payments made
- Any Other business related expenses
- Any Health insurances
- Any Premiums that are paid to cover the sole-proprietor and family
- Any Premiums that are paid on behalf of partners and S corporation shareholders
- Any Information on spouse's employer provided insurance

Remember that this is not an exhaustive list and you might have to account for some other necessary papers as well.

Chapter 9

Things to Do When You Can't Pay Taxes in A Year

Many times, companies are unable to come up with enough finances to pay taxes. Despite being common, it is not at all a healthy situation for any company to be in as the IRS can be unforgiving.

Most companies have an inherent fear of the IRS which forces them to set aside a certain sum that they wish to contribute towards taxes, even if it means eating away into their profits. But this is only justified given how the IRS can turn the company upside down to tumble out change.

However, if for some unfortunate reasons you are unable to pay for taxes at all then there are some things that you can do to placate the situation. In this chapter, we will look at some of them in detail.

Grace time

The first and possibly most important step to take is to ask for grace time from the IRS. This might sound extremely rudimentary but is the best solution to this problem. You can ask for some grace time so as to come up with enough finances to pay the taxes. The IRS generally grants 60 to 120 days grace time to a company to raise finances for taxes.

Borrow

It is a good idea for you to borrow the sum from a family member. You can regard it as a loan and borrow the precise amount that needs to be paid to the IRS. You and your family member will both benefit from it, as they will earn a higher rate of interest from the loan than they would from a savings account. You, on the other hand, will be able to pay the IRS on time and avoid a lot of unwanted problems. But make sure you specify that it is a loan that you have taken from the relative and it is not a gift. You have to submit papers that say you will be paying them an interest on the borrowed sum.

Benefactor

You actually might find a benefactor to help you pay your dues to the IRS. This might sound a little impossible for those that have not approached someone influential before, but if you approach the right person then you might be able to raise enough finance to pay your taxes.

Pay a little

It is best to always pay a little money upfront. Once you are granted the grace time, you can make a little advance payment to convince them that you will be paying the entire amount in due course of time. The amount need not be too big and can be just a small percentage of what you owe to the IRS. Consider paying the amount in cash, as that will be much better than paying using cards. This will also help you reduce the penalty that you might have to pay later for your delayed tax payments.

Credit card

If you really don't have a way to raise enough money for taxes but really want to be done with it on time, then you can consider paying with your credit card. The IRS accepts plastic money. Don't worry, you won't be charged extra for choosing this mode of payment, however, the company filing for you might charge you. You might have to part with a certain sum to be paid for the commission. You can use up to 2 cards per person, which is great as you can possibly pay the entire amount. However, don't make this your go to option every time. You cannot run your business and then charge tax on your credit cards. You have to put in efforts to better your business output in order to pay tax the right way.

Refinancing

You can consider refinancing your home. If you have a home of your own, then you can consider refinancing it and use the equity to deduct taxes. You can use refinanced equity to deduct from your income tax, which is not possible with credit card finance. Look for a low mortgage rate that will help you finish paying up within a short period of time. Again, remember that this can only be done once.

Installments

A rather convenient way of paying your taxes is through the installment method. Yes, that's correct; you can pay your taxes to the IRS by choosing the installment method, which will allow you to break up the total sum into small parts. But remember that you will have to pay a little extra as fine. You will have to calculate how much you will be charged as fine. But it will be well worth it, as you will have enough time to make the full and final payment. But there is a limit on using this method, as it is only applicable to those that don't owe the IRS more than $50,000 in taxes.

Negotiate

If all else fails and you are just not able to pay the taxes, then you can negotiate with the IRS. You can ask them to reduce the amount of tax that you need to pay. But before you present the plea, you have to craft a proper proposal. Remember that the IRS rejects nearly 80% of the pleas and so; you have just a 20% chance at making this work. You can speak with an expert and seek appropriate advice. You can also tag your tax preparer along as he might have some valuable insights into it. You have to put your negotiating skills to the ultimate test as you have to convince the IRS that you have no other means to pay the taxes in full.

Call for help

As an ultimate last resort, you can consider calling the IRS to seek guidance with your problem. If for some reason you are absolutely unable to come up with ways in which you can actually make a payment of your taxes, then the IRS will surely be help you out in that regard. They will attend your call and tell you what exactly you can do about it. Here is the number to call: 1.800.829.1040. You can call them to seek a solution to your problem.

These form the different things that you can do to avoid paying heavy fines by defaulting to pay taxes for your company.

General taxation mistakes to avoid

Here are some taxation mistakes that you need to avoid in order to make the most of your profits.

Ignoring software

There are many software and websites out there that will help you get started with your tax filings on the right foot. You have to use them to have a smooth journey. Some of the best websites include TurboTax, which provides free advice and also helps people file their taxes. You can also make use of record keeping applications to maintain your company's records. You will be able to retrieve the information on time and find it easy to file your tax returns.

Quarterly taxes

Do not forget to file your quarterly taxes. For the first year of business, most companies get a free quarterly tax pass but will be held accountable for it from the next year onwards. You have to well verse yourself with what needs to be done and the rules that apply to your type of company. You can go through all the rules in detail to see if you qualify to pay quarterly taxes. Even if you don't, many experts advise company owners to pay up their dues to avoid hassles later.

Filing in a hurry

It has been harped upon enough times before and probably is the most important thing to remember when you wish to file for taxes. You have to prepare for it well in advance and remain ready to file your taxes on time. If you remain in a hurry to get done with everything then you are surely bound to make mistakes. Remain calm and patient and in the right frame of mind. You don't have to lose sleep over filing your taxes and must think of it as a business chore.

Not availing help

Remember that filing individual income taxes can in itself be quite confusing and then add to it the complications that company taxes bring along. So, it is best for you to employ a professional who will be able to help you pay taxes on time. It can get a bit painful to do everything by yourself, especially if you have not filed taxes before. So, it is best to employ a professional tax preparer to avoid being left with a bitter taste in your mouth.

Mixing finances

It has been mentioned several times in this book that most sole proprietors commingle their personal and professional finances. However, this might not always be the best thing to do. Mixing finances might cause you to get confused and not know how much you need to file. In fact, your work will double or triple as you will have to individually separate all the different expenses and incomes that you have accrued. It is best for you to maintain separate accounts for each type.

Miscalculations

The worst thing that you can do while filing for tax is, miscalculate how much you owe to the IRS. If you are not a numbers kind of person or have no practical knowledge about math whatsoever, then please enlist the help of an expert. You might be great at running a business, but getting the math part wrong can cause you to part with more money than necessary. Calculating correctly but adding in an extra "o" can also spell trouble. So be present in the moment when you are making the calculations and also when you are recording it.

Names/addresses

It is vital for you to get the names and addresses of your company and yourself right. If there is even a small mistake like the addition or deduction of a single letter, then it will spell trouble for you. You must ensure that everything is clearly mentioned and that you have checked it twice. You have to also ensure that your spouse's name is added in correctly along with the right surname.

Identification number

Don't forget to mention your identification number, as it is important to specify what company you are running. The IRS has seized appending your social security number, which means that you have to make use of your identification number to tell them who you are. The tax id number is a 9-digit code that needs to be added in while filing your tax returns.

Donations

Some business owners don't understand that donations can be deducted from tax filings. So, remember to mention clearly all the donations that you have been making to various organizations through the year. Whether they are cash donations or other donations, you have to mention their value clearly. Remember that any clothing or other items that you donate need to be in pristine condition. If they don't meet the requirements, then the IRS has the power to cancel the deductions. You have to mention clearly everything that you have donated and where it has been dispatched.

Online sign

Don't forget to sign digitally. If you are filing taxes on online, then you have to make use of a digital signature to identify yourself. Just like you would sign with a pen on the papers, you have to punch in your unique 9-digit code to identify yourself.

These form the different taxation mistakes that you have to avoid in order to prevent any problems.

Chapter 10

Tax Breaks & Loopholes

A Few Big Corporate Tax Breaks

U.S. companies — in the same way as other Americans — misuse each accessible rule in the tax code to lessen the taxes they disburse. The United States has one of the most noteworthy corporate tax rates on the planet, at 35 percent (excluding any state levies), yet the real sum in corporate taxes that the government accumulates ("the swaying tax rate") is underneath those of Germany, Japan, Canada, and China, among others.

The reason is stunningly permitted "tax expenditures," which is a doublespeak term intended to legitimize uncommon tax breaks and loopholes. Those "consumptions" will cost the U.S. government $628.6 billion throughout the following five years, as indicated by a 2010 report from the Tax Foundation. With guidance from the Urban Institute's Eric Toder, one of the nation's preeminent powers on corporate tax approach, we have summarized the 10 most immoderate corporate tax escape clauses, and who will profit from them.

Deferral of Income from Prescribed Foreign Corporations

Under this law, multinational organizations can put off paying U.S. income taxes until they exchange overseas earnings back to the United States. Practically speaking, numerous organizations leave quite a bit of their benefits abroad for inconclusive periods of time, and because of this end up paying just the tax in the applicable remote nation, which is likely far lower than the U.S. rate, and thus avoiding U.S. taxes for an indefinite amount of time. The list of companies utilizing this loophole is incredibly long.

5-yr Cost to Government: $172.1 billion

Who benefits: Every multinational organization

Barring of Interest on State & Local Bonds

Organizations (and people) don't pay the federal income tax on income from their interests in state and civil bonds. Besides, organizations can at times issue tax-free bonds of their own for ventures that benefit the general population, for example the development of an airport, stadium or hospitals.

<u>5-yr Cost to Government</u>: $59.8 billion

<u>Who benefits</u>: High-salary investors & companies.

Deduction for National Manufacturing

This loophole makes a tax deduction possible for business exercises led by American organizations inside the United States. It covers ordinary makers and additionally stretches out to include businesses like software development and film production companies. The expectation is to continue producing in the U.S. rather than being outsourced.

<u>5-yr Cost to Government</u>: $58 billion

<u>Who benefits</u>: Any U.S. organization that delivers a product inside U.S. borders.

Accelerated Depreciation of Machinery & Equipment

This tax break permits organizations to deduct the majority of the deterioration of a physical asset without a moment's delay (rather than over the, say, 20 years it really takes the item to devalue) as depreciation. This is what might as well be called the U.S. government giving the organization a kind of advance on future tax break amounts. Since 2011, Congress has made this tax break option significantly bigger in order to empower interest in hardware development.

5-yr Cost to Government: $51.7 billion

Who benefits: Airlines & producers utilizing a large amount of physical gear that lasts for numerous years.

Credit for Low-Income Housing Investments

As you may imagine, this one presents tax breaks to organizations that build low-income housing developments. This tax break puts aside 20% to 40% of the cost for developing a variety of new housing units for individuals whose wage is well beneath the area's average gross pay.

5-yr Cost to Government: $34.5 billion

Who benefits: Real estate developers.

Alcohol Fuel Credit

This is a tax credit for the creation of alcohol based fuel, most usually ethanol, which is produced using corn. The credit extends from $0.39 to $0.60 per gallon. In principle, the credit is intended to incentivize creating alternative energy options from imported oil. It is to a great extent also a tax which props up the cost of corn and is to a great degree well known in corn-growing states such as Iowa and Illinois.

5-yr Cost to Government: $32 billion

Who benefits: Food & agricultural firms in the Midwest.

Deferred Taxes for Financial Institutions on Precise Income Earned Overseas

Since most financial institutions lead their remote operations as branches as opposed to as backups, as most organizations in different commercial ventures do, they don't profit by the tax breaks offered to outside auxiliaries. To make up for this, this loophole empowers firms to treat the money paid as wages in their outside overseas branches as though they were backups, in addition to the majority of the common tax breaks.

5-yr Cost to Government: $29.9 billion

Who benefits: Any money related firms with remote operations.

Research & Experimentation Tax Credit

Expected to promote research work inside of organizations in its simplest form, this break takes into consideration a 20 percent tax credit for expenditures that are termed "qualified research outlays." There are more complicated applications at the same time as well. Critics grumble that it is paying corporations to do research that would have been needed to be conducted anyway.

5-yr Cost to Government: *$29.8 billion*

Who benefits: Pharmaceutical organizations, cutting edge organizations, engineers, agribusiness conglomerates.

Inventory Property Sales

Overseas profits of American organizations are taxed in the nation in which they're created, and the U.S. gives a tax credit for that sum with the specific end goal of avoiding double taxation. A few organizations have accumulated an excess amount of such tax credits (the "inventory"), and with a specific end goal to utilize them completely, they misleadingly facilitate outside pay by way of a "title section rule" to authorize organizations to designate 50 percent of wages paid from the U.S. creation of its products that are sold in another nation as salary produced by that remote nation (the "property sales").

5-yr Cost to Government: **$16.7** billion

Who benefits: Multinational companies with operations in high-tax remote nations.

Graduated Corporate Income

This approach puts the main $50,000 of a corporation's profit at a 15 percent tax rate with higher benefits levels. The tax rate then increases proportionately according to the profit and peaks at 35 percent with taxable corporate salary surpassing $335,000. The outcome is that a proprietor of a small enterprise pays just 15 percent in taxes on the main $50,000 of profit, which then conceivably leaves the remaining amount for reinvestment and development.

5-yr Cost to Government (2011-2015): $16.4 billion

Who benefits: Individuals that claim to own a small business.

Small Business Tax Loopholes You Should Make The Most Of

As any proprietor can bear witness to, developing and keeping up small business profits is a steady fight. Be that as it may, by comprehension and use of some business-accommodating tax loopholes, tenacious small business entrepreneurs can discover approaches that will keep a significantly greater amount of their well-deserved capital in the company. Following is a look at five legitimate tax loopholes and tax breaks that can be a major help for small business entrepreneurs.

The Remunerations of S Corporation Status

S Corporation status can be a noteworthy cash saver for small entrepreneurs who are now working for profitable and lucrative organizations. A proprietor of an S Corporation can financially take part in the business through wages and "profits." Business proprietors can set wages for themselves and their workers at Fair Market Value and pay the rest of benefits as a profit, which is not subject to the 15% payroll tax.

For instance, if an S Corporation makes $100,000 every year in benefits, yet pays out just $40,000 of that benefit in wages, the Corporation spares $9,000 every year by not paying the 15% tax on the remaining $60,000 paid out of profits.

Controlling State Tax Nexus

A few states have a considerably better business-accommodating tax code than others, and understanding which activities build up tax nexus (adequate physical nearness to required tax installments) and which don't in a given state can permit organizations to abstain from paying higher state taxes.

State tax laws fluctuate from state-to-state, yet by abstaining from owning property in a specific state, having representatives in a specific state, and/or brokering deals in a specific state, you can be able to abstain from setting up unfavorable tax nexus in that state.

Withhold Medical Taxes through a Medical Reimbursement Plan

Out-of-pocket medical costs are ordinarily not a tax-deductible item. In any case, entrepreneurs can actualize a Medical Reimbursement Plan and have the business repay every single restorative tax. By using this loophole, non-deductible medicinal costs turn out to be lawfully seen as operational tax.

Family Income Splitting

Family salary splitting is another legal, simple, and honest route for small entrepreneurs to abstain from paying higher tax rates on high-margin wages. Here's a model of how enrolling a young boy or girl can cut taxes.

In the event that a small business entrepreneur makes $70,000 every year in pay, the greater part of the pay above $37,450 will be taxed at the 25% level of pay. In any case, by paying $35,000 of that salary to a young boy or girl representative of the business (who can then utilize it for everyday costs and school education cost, for instance), the greater part of the $70,000 wage will be taxed at a 15% rate or lower.

Subtract Vacation Outlay as a Business Tax

By arranging vacations in a joint effort with business travel or the other way around, the travel cost connected with an excursion can become tax deductible. For specific organizations, this strategy has exactly the intended effect.

For instance, if a small business entrepreneur might want a tax deductible flight to Las Vegas, he or she possibly will formulate a lowball tender on a small portion of business land in the Las Vegas zone in the interest of the business.

In an ideal situation, the business could secure a decent parcel of land from a merchant who is urgently trying to dispose of it at an under the market cost. But even if your lowball offer is dismissed, as expected, the excursion to Vegas is still lawfully a business trip, and the cost of the flight and hotel room can be deducted as an operational tax.

Takeaway

These examples are only five of the ways that a small business entrepreneur can exploit opportunities that are available to him or her in the tax code. Be that as it may, this last point is essential: proper arranging and strict abiding of obligatory regulations in order to profit from these loopholes is a noteworthy legal undertaking that no small business entrepreneur ought to endeavor without the insight of a tax expert.

Illustrations of a Few Astounding Corporate Tax Loopholes

Many organizations have been making an immense financial profit due to our present tax laws. The American tax framework frequently appears to be unjustifiable. Most individuals assume that their tax rates are too high and that others are not sufficiently paying. Many people only think of loopholes as illegal ways for well-off individuals to avoid paying tax, such as the use of offshore tax shelters. Outrage about injustice in tax reaches into the corporate world as well. Some of these accusations are justifiable, and following are a number of ways organizations have been exploiting our present tax laws.

#1 One especially unfortunate corporate loophole successfully compensates organizations for an offense. At the point when organizations get sued, they are permitted to deduct the amount they need lay out to cover the harm done by casualties from their taxable income. As a result, this strengths taxpayers to partake in the budgetary aftermath of their activities.

As though this wasn't terrible enough, organizations can even deduct punitive damages that juries or judges levy with the specific end goal of hindering organizations from repeating similar illegal conduct at a later point in time. Punitive damages are frequently the largest financial percentage of harms included in a claim, and the bigger the sum, the more prominent the tax savings funds will be in connection with paying the punitive damages.

However, there are a few kinds of transgressions that organizations can't deduct. Criminal fines and punishments owed to the government aren't qualified, and settlements that describe installments as criminal punishments for tax rationales aren't tax deductible. Still, notwithstanding intermittent endeavors to change the law, organizations keep on enjoying the tax deductible status for a hefty portion of their lawful liabilities — even when they are found guilty as charged by a court of law.

#2 One of the world's biggest cruise lines posted a profit of $1.2 billion, yet it only has to pay $9 million in income taxes. According to these numbers, its financial tax rate for the year was under 1%. This is no mistake, and it also isn't an aftereffect of former year's fatalities. Cruise lines successfully skirt any U.S. corporate income taxes that you would expect them to pay. On account of invaluable tax arrangements, cruise lines like Carnival make their homes in Panama and different locales, making them outside organizations that essentially get, for the most part, American travelers. In Carnival's situation, just a small portion of its wages paid out for its Alaskan Tours is taxable under U.S. corporate tax law.

You'd be pardoned for thinking Carnival is an American organization. All things considered, its biggest office is situated in Miami. There you will discover a large portion of its shore side representatives, from credit card scam experts to corporate officials. However, what you won't discover at the American workplaces is a tax bill; Carnival and numerous other travel lines are organized to guarantee that their benefits aren't American, regardless of the fact that their operations are mainly.

#3 Does paying your income tax sometimes make you as angry as a raging bull? If it does, this next loophole will really get going. Some organizations get an executioner tax break by way of a technique normally known as tax inversion bargains. A tax inversion occurs when a residential organization buys a remote organization in a nation with a lower peripheral corporate tax rate than the United States, and after that redomiciles its base camp in the outside nation.

The United States' crest peripheral corporate tax of 40% is the second-most noteworthy on the planet, so it's invaluable for some U.S.-based organizations to buy similarly measured organizations in abroad markets to bring down their successful tax rate. The greater the organization, the more sizable the tax break will be. Take, for instance, the buyout of Allergan by Pfizer. Despite the new U.S. Treasury Department regulations that endeavor to limit tax inversion bargains, Allergan shareholders will in any case claim more than 40% of the joined entity, and Pfizer is paying for the arrangement with Pfizer shares (11.3 Pfizer shares for each Allergan share, to be exact).

At the end of the day, the arrangement may eventually no longer be possible due to new guidelines that can be put out by the Treasury Department. As it stands for now, however, the afore mentioned merger will lower Pfizer's operative tax rate from 25% to somewhere around 17% and 18% per year, and will probably spare the organization more than $1 billion in any operational collaborations that are handled. Regardless of legislators' earnest attempts, tax inversion bargains remain a smart way for organizations, predominantly healthcare firms, to cut their tax obligation and hold on to a greater amount of their benefits.

#4- Many large American organizations are choosing not to bring home income they produce abroad for the very reason that it will then be taxed. According to a few studies, more than $2 trillion is being put away abroad and not brought back to the US, which implies that more than $600 billion in taxes is not being gathered. That $600 billion would go far in America, wouldn't you say? It could pay for a lot of framework repairs, and help get the country out of debt.

However, what these organizations are currently doing is not illegal, and some would contend that they're serving their shareholders well by spending less on taxes. Be that as it may, there is also a drawback to this method, as cash not brought home can't be spent here for further development — including areas such as R&D, extra laborers, advertising, or acquisitions. Numerous companies will say that the US current corporate tax rate of 35% is too high, however, others have called attention to the fact that on account of different tax breaks and loopholes, several enterprises pay far below 35% — and that partnerships' share of the nation's aggregate taxable income was as of late only 9%, which is far lower than the 33% it was in 1950. However, as long as foreign tax rates stay more favorable than U.S. tax rates, we will continue to see companies go this route as long as it remains legal.

Without a doubt, numerous organizations pay little or nothing in taxes. As per a study by Taxpayers for Tax Justice, organizations including General Electric, Mattel, Qualcomm, JetBlue Airways, Prudential Financial, and Xerox paid under 10% in taxes in 2014. Taking this into consideration, the American corporate tax rate is significantly lowered by the more favorable tax rates found at global midpoints.

Tax Loopholes that Predominantly Benefit the Rich

A tax loophole isn't unlawful. It just appears that the individual profiting from the loophole is regularly taking after the letter of the tax law instead of abiding by the spirit of the law. So also, there are numerous tax deductions that seem to give unbalanced tax cuts to a chosen few. Here are a few tax breaks that fall into those classes.

Capital Additions Tax Rate

The present 15 percent capital additions tax rate for the majority of investors with a zero percent rate for lower income taxpayers are part of the period tax breaks from the time of George W. Hedge. The thought behind the reasoning that lower capital increases tax is that it energizes venture, which makes new firms that will contract extra individuals — all of us have benefited at one point or another on account of this tax-subsidized speculation chain. Let's reconsider it, though. This tax loophole is evaluated by the Joint Committee on Taxation to have cost the U.S. Treasury about $457 billion from 2011 to 2015.

If prosperous people such as notable financier Warren Buffet were to pay a more generous tax amount, it could bring down general tax rates significantly, which is an incredibly motivating factor. Buffett's oft-rehashed admission that his tax rate is lower than his secretary's started the most recent political level headed discussion on the decency of lowering tax rates on small business ventures. Middle class taxpayers usually pay tax on their earnings at usual pay tax rates equal to 35 percent.

The truly rich, in any case, are unique in relation to you and me in that they tend to profit through speculations rather than standard paychecks — meaning the greater part of their cash is taxed at 15 percent. However, shouldn't something be said about the brilliant zero tax rate for investors in the 10 percent and 15 percent salary tax sections? Most people at those tax levels don't have a great deal, if any money left over to contribute in the wake of paying their bills. Yet, by giving them the alternative, Congress felt it was still more beneficial to vote on the side of a tax break that benefits principally the rich.

Home Loan Interest Inference

In the event that you've ever purchased a house, one of the principal things your real estate agent and mortgage broker most likely called your attention to was that you get the opportunity to deduct your house credit's home loan interest on your taxes. What they didn't let you know was that your tax break is endorsed by most property holders who don't get this tax break. The home loan interest derivation is the biggest individual taxpayer to the U.S.

Treasury. Uncle Sam lost an expected $464 billion between 2011 and 2015.

Moreover, that sum is racked up by a mere third of American taxpayers who organize. An even worse aspect, according to financial analysts, is that the tax break likely isn't fundamental to the decision to purchase a home. Most other industrialized countries worldwide don't offer their populace a tax reduction for acquiring a house, but these people still purchase homes. No individual has ever purchased or not purchased their main home solely due to the fact that they will or will not receive a tax break. What market analysts say that the home loan interest truly does, is energize all the more fiscally well-off people to purchase more homes and increase their real estate portfolios.

In July 2011, an analysis, "Unmasking the Mortgage Interest Deduction," established that the yearly standard deduction of the home loan derivation for a taxpayer making $50,000 to $75,000 was a mere $179, and that just around 33% in this group actually claim the deduction. At the upper pay level, nonetheless, mortgage holders with salaries surpassing $200,000 get a yearly tax break of more than $2,200, and right around 75% claim the deduction. The home loan interest deduction deductions are likewise socially unbalanced.

As high-wage taxpayers receive more in return, so do metropolitan territories with high salaries, taxes, and lodging costs. That traditionally has had a tendency to exist especially in districts in California and also the Northeast. Consequently, whenever you visit your cousin at his new house in New Jersey, ensure he expresses gratitude towards you for your assistance with his home purchase.

Second Home Loan Interest Deduction

Not to continue singling out property holders, but there is yet another residential deduction that needs to be cut: the credit for interest on a summer home. Of course, there are some owners of second homes that are a long way from being rich. Be that as it may, the individuals who claim a ski chalet in Aspen, Colo., a sea view getaway along the Miami's South Beach, or a pied-a-terre in New York City in which to rest following a late Broadway premiere night, more often than not are rich.

What's more, they get the opportunity to discount the interest on those pricey second homes as a separate deduction for home loan debt as high as $1 million. Even more astonishing is the fact that proprietors of opulent yachts can deduct mortgage interest on credits they took out to purchase their smaller than normal Queen Marys, as well. The Internal Revenue Code states a vessel can be viewed as a home as long as it has sleeping quarters, a kitchen and a lavatory. The home designation rules likewise imply that recreational vehicles could be eligible as residences, giving proprietors of those extravagant transports an additional tax deduction, as well.

Of course there are a few individuals who do live in houseboats. In light of the fact that the deduction applies to a wide range of second-home alternatives, supporters of the tax cut contend that it is reasonable. However, the tax code would be considerably more pleasant if single property holders were not forced to sponsor any second homes.

Conceded Interest Unique Tax Treatment

Do you remember the discussion over lower tax rates that Republican ex-presidential hopeful and previous Massachusetts Gov. Mitt Romney paid? A fraction of the amount was a direct outcome of his capital returns on ventures. However, Romney additionally got some pay for his work at Bain Capital. A tax loophole permits that pay to be taxed at a lower rate. The administrators of most private equity reserves get a rate of the net returns as an administrative fee.

This installment is identified as carried interest, and here is its delightful aspect: carried interest is not taxed like the general interest most taxpayers get on standard bank accounts. It is instead taxed as a capital return. That implies while consistent interest received from most taxpayers with their bank accounts is taxed at rates that could go up to 35 percent, people who receive carried interest installments owe a present top rate of 15 percent on that income.

A Bloomberg Global Poll in January found that 66% of survey respondents said the carried interest tax cut is not beneficial. That is predictable with the survey's finding on the subject in the United States, where 67% said the lower tax rate isn't reasonable. A bill was presented in Congress to change the tax treatment of the equity fund managers' profit. Of course, it still needs to be acted upon.

Tax Breaks for Offshoring US Occupations

The capacity to save money on corporate taxes by transporting operations abroad is one of the most attacked corporate tax cuts. Yes, organizations can cut tax costs by migrating abroad. The tax cut is not extraordinary in the case of moving, say, an industrial facility and its 600 employments from St. Louis to Singapore. Furthermore, according to the Tax Foundation, occupations are no less than three times more inclined to move, starting with moving one state, then onto the next, and then abroad. Still, when U.S. unemployment is high, a tax cut that recompenses moving additional employment offshore appears to be a bad idea.

Will these, along with some other individual and corporate tax loopholes, tax breaks, and as the government calls them, tax spending, be wiped out or even changed at all? Currently is isn't likely. Every single one is entirely lobbied for by the groups that acquire its benefits. Additionally, these companies and individuals are generally the same people who have a tendency to contribute liberally to political battles. However, while it isn't likely, it still shouldn't be entirely discounted

Key Highlights

Taxation can seem like a complicated subject to deal with, but it is easier than you think to file taxes. Many company owners dread the thought of having to file for income tax and wonder if there is a way to escape from it, however, there is no way to escape from taxes and you have to make it a compulsory part of your expenditure.

We looked at the different types of taxes that are levied at different levels. Each of them is just as important as the other and you have to try and understand each individually. It is quite simple to understand federal taxes, as they are universally applicable. But state and city taxes will differ from place to place.

Sole proprietors refer to people that single handedly own and operate a business. Sole proprietors are taxed like how regular income tax payers are charged. They have to fill out Form 1040 Schedule C or C-EZ and additionally Schedule F for a farm business. Most sole proprietors mix their personal and professional accounts that make it easier for them to keep track of their incomes and expenses.

LLCs are companies whose members' liabilities are limited. So, in case they forget to pay their company tax, the owners will not be held liable for it. LLCs can be treated as sole proprietors, partnerships or corporations. All of these will be individually taxed in different ways.

You have the chance to employ a professional tax preparer. He or she should have relevant experience in preparing and filing taxes. A professional tax preparer is generally chosen based on their qualifications and how many taxes they have successfully filed. You have to put in efforts to find the right taxpayer for yourself and ensure that you are ready with your tax papers on time.

There is a deadline to pay your taxes. You have to file within April 15th and can seek an extension of up to April 18th or 20th. In rare cases the IRS can extend it by 60 or 120 days. This is grace time that is given to a company that is simply unable to come up with appropriate finances in time to pay taxes.

There are many things that you can do to save on the amount of taxes that you have to pay to the IRS. We looked at the different types of investments that you can make with your money and considerably reduce the amount that you pay as taxes. You can go through it again if you wish to understand it better.

The taxpayers check list will help you prepare to file your taxes with ease. The checklist, however, might not be exhaustive and you might have to ready certain additional papers along with the ones mentioned. You must keep a record of all and can hold soft copies of each.

Many companies dread the IRS and for good reason. However, you have to stand up to them in case they have made a mistake in filing your returns. You must also try your best to remain in their good books at all times to avoid unnecessary tiffs.

We looked at the different taxation mistakes that you must avoid while filing taxes for your startups, LLCs or sole proprietor businesses. You can go through it again if you wish to understand it better and avoid them.

Lastly, remember to keep all your records up to date. When you sit down to file for returns, you cannot run around looking for important receipts. You have to have them ready and updated.

Tax Tactics for Small Business Entrepreneurs

In case you're maintaining your own business, making sure you have enough time to keep up with cash saving tax systems can be a trying task — one that is very involved due to the way that tax laws are continually evolving.

Run the Numbers

The best thing you can do before the end of the year is getting your bookkeeping organized and figuring out whether you have a profit or loss. It's best to do that now, while you still have room in your schedule to make changes. If you don't plan ahead, you may be in trouble. I've seen too many individuals come to me and say, "Look, I have a $100,000 deficit for the year" — simply to find out that the entrepreneur has neglected to accurately represent something, such as the value of stock. When it's correctly entered, they may find out that they actually have a $200,000 profit and owe tax, and then it might be past the point in the year when it is still possible to make a change, because they didn't discover the error until April 13.

On the off-chance that you haven't procured a tax expert, one choice to survey your tax circumstance is to sign into one of the tax-preparation sites, for example, H&R Block, TurboTax, or one of the others, in order to run the numbers. However, you will be utilizing out of date programming, but it will still be superior to the tax estimating instruments that the vast majority of the organizations offer. Simply enter the numbers that identify your present year's salary and costs, so you can really see what the genuine potential taxes are, including the impact of the taxes that are more often than not disregarded in quickie calculators.

Self-employment taxes can be a major surprise. You think you may have no tax to pay because your business benefit is $30,000 but your separated deductions are also around $30,000, but then you find out that you are still getting hit with self-employment taxes on the full $30,000. That can turn into an enormous surprise for individuals.

Exploit Terminating Procurements

There's no real way to anticipate how the U.S. Congress will act. Frequently, terminating tax procurements should be done looking at least a year into the future, however it is difficult to know if those procurements will still be available at that time. It is always wise to survey whether any business choices you make can be customized to exploit tax breaks now. For instance, the supposed Section 179 expense deduction at present permits small organizations to discount the tax of specific sorts of hardware purchasing — both new and used — up to $500,000. Come January, that tax break is slated to drop to $25,000. Make sure to educate yourself ahead of time.

Congress has a tendency to limit tax cuts, but if you never identify it, you may not take advantage of the tax cut until after it drops from $500,000 down to $25,000, which will make you lose a significant amount of money. You should also look unto what is known as a half reward devaluation tax break that permits entrepreneurs to deduct up to half of the tax of specific acquisitions — and there's no dollar limit.

The property must be new, and must be put in service by Dec. 31.

You will still have to act quickly on such purchasing. That tax cut is additionally set to terminate towards the end of the year and will likely not be extended. Entrepreneurs who are taking a gander at a major benefit this year ought to consider making buys now, as opposed to one year from this time. Simply buy what you were planning on purchasing next year now, and start using it before the end of the year to make sure you get the tax break.

One more terminating procurement to consider — depending on your business circumstance — is the Work Opportunity tax credit, which is accessible to entrepreneurs who enlist veterans, disabled individuals, and individuals in other select groups. The tax credit, for the most part, is worth up to 40% of the principal $6,000 of qualified wages paid to another contract who can be categorized as one of the specified groups. (The exact measure of the credit fluctuates taking into account various aspects.) In this case you would need to hire someone from one of the specified groups before the end of the year in order to take advantage of the tax break.

Evaluate your Circumstance under the Affordable Care Act

While small managers — those with less than 50 representatives — aren't liable to penalties on the off chance that they don't give protection to their laborers, you might be qualified for a tax credit that has been obtainable since 2010 if you offer health benefits anyway. More information about this can be found at www.IRS.gov. Additionally, some small organizations might be required to tell their workers about the medical coverage accessible to them through the new healthcare exchanges. For the most part, this prerequisite is restricted to organizations that produce at any rate higher than $500,000 in yearly dollar volume.

Conclusion

When you are managing a small business, a fundamental awareness of the tax laws, the various business types and allowable deductions are an important part of your business, despite the fact that you will most likely hire a tax or accounting professional to do the work. The amount you pay and the deductions you can take will depend on what you gross, your business type and whether or not you have a certain amount of employees.

As a small business holder, you will have to become accustomed to federal business taxes. You may not want to pay them, but they are a requirement and should be built into the structure of your business.

I thank you once again for choosing this book and hope you had a good time reading it.

The main aim of this book was to educate you on the topic of taxes that companies have to pay to the IRS.

Whether you are a startup, an LLC or a sole proprietor, you have to pay your taxes on time to avoid fines.

It is never advisable to evade taxes, as that can land you in unnecessary trouble. You have to ensure that you pay all your dues on time, and start preparing for it well in advance so as to avoid rushing it at the last minute.

If you still have any doubts on the topic, then you can go through this book again and clear them away. You can also turn to other sources for further reference and equip yourself with the knowledge to pay your taxes on time.

I wish you luck and hope you fill out all the forms and file your company's tax with ease.

Made in the USA
Middletown, DE
28 July 2016